KATE RIGGS

grow with me

LADYBUG

CREATIVE EDUCATION

Published by Creative Education
P.O. Box 227, Mankato, Minnesota 56002
Creative Education is an imprint of
The Creative Company
www.thecreativecompany.us

Design and production by Ellen Huber
Art direction by Rita Marshall
Printed in the United States of America

Photographs by 123rf (Ivan Mikhaylov), Animals Animals
(Donald Specker), Bigstock (mbridger, South12th),
Biosphoto (Samuel Dhier, Yvette Tavernier, Claudius
Thiriet), Dreamstime (Graemo, Ivan Mikhaylov,
Pakhnyushchyy), Getty Images (Dorling Kindersley,
Sebastian Kennerknecht, Martin Ruegner, Kees Smans,
Stockbyte, Dmitri Vervitsiotis, Visuals Unlimited, Inc./
Nigel Cattlin, amanda vivan), iStockphoto (Eric Isselée,
David Orr, Tomasz Pietryszek), Photo Researchers
(George D. Lepp, Perennou Nuridsany, James H.
Robinson), SuperStock (Mauritius), Veer (dabjola,
defun, dngood, irin-k, newleaf)

Library of Congress Cataloging-in-Publication Data
Riggs, Kate.
Ladybug / Kate Riggs.
p. cm. — (Grow with me)
Includes bibliographical references and index.
Summary: An exploration of the life cycle and life span
of ladybugs, using up-close photographs and step-by-
step text to follow a ladybug's growth process from egg
to larva to pupa to mature insect.

ISBN 978-1-60818-217-6
1. Ladybugs—Life cycles—Juvenile literature. I. Title.
QL596.C65R54 2012
595.76'9—dc23   2011040500

First Edition
9 8 7 6 5 4 3 2 1

TABLE OF CONTENTS

Ladybugs are insects. Insects have six legs and one or two pairs of wings. Ladybugs have just one pair of wings. Their wings and legs are connected to the part of their body called the **thorax**.

head

thorax

abdomen

4

Ladybugs live in forests, grasslands, fields, and gardens. There are about 5,000 **species** of ladybug. They do not have nests or **permanent** homes. Ladybugs that live in places where winters are cold take shelter in people's houses. If they stay warm enough, they can survive the winter.

Ladybugs belong to the beetle family and are sometimes called "lady beetles."

Ladybug eggs stick to the leaf and stand upright.

6

These ladybug eggs were laid in the middle of a bunch of aphids.

7

Female ladybugs lay their eggs on or under plant leaves. A ladybug can lay 10 to 20 eggs at a time. The eggs are all in a group called a cluster. Ladybug eggs look like tiny yellow or orange jellybeans.

Some ladybug species lay just one cluster of eggs. Some lay many clusters each year. Mother ladybugs lay their eggs near large groups of **aphids**, **mites**, and other soft-bodied creatures that eat plants. These are what ladybugs like to eat the most.

Inside the egg, a ladybug **larva** is growing. It grows for three to seven days. Ladybug eggs need to be warm to hatch. It can take longer for them to hatch if the temperature is too cold. This is because ladybugs are cold-blooded. They cannot keep their bodies warm if the temperature around them is not also warm.

8

Just before an egg hatches, it turns a gray color. The larva that comes out looks like a tiny alligator! A ladybug larva is black with bright spots. It has a spiny back. Larvae can eat aphids and mites as soon as they hatch.

The seven-spotted ladybug hatches from its egg (opposite) and starts exploring (pictured).

10 *Ladybug larvae may look a little scary, but they do not harm people.*

A larva spends all day eating food. Larvae can eat about 25 aphids a day. A larva that hatches in the spring or summer spends two to four weeks eating.

Larvae shed their skin, or molt, as they grow. This happens three or four times. Molting helps a larva develop the body it will need as a ladybug.

11

This ladybug larva has just molted and is growing a new skin.

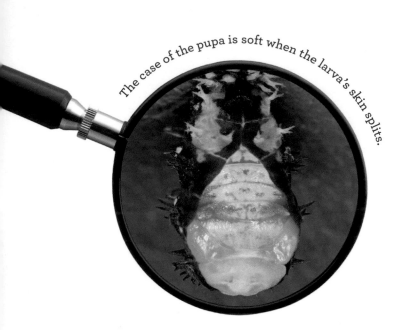

The case of the pupa is soft when the larva's skin splits.

12 After it has finished growing, a larva looks for a place to rest. It attaches itself under a leaf or on a stem. Then it hangs upside down. After about two days, the larva's skin splits down the back. Inside is a **pupa**.

The pupa is about the size of an adult ladybug. But it is wrapped up and protected in a case. The pupa looks a little bit like a small shrimp.

No matter what stage they are in, from larva to adult, ladybugs move slowly.

An adult seven-spotted
ladybug's body is
0.3 inches (7.6 mm) long.

14

A pupa goes through a process of change called metamorphosis (*met-ah-MORE-foh-sis*). This word means "change shape."

After five to seven days, metamorphosis is usually complete. The pupa breaks out of the case. The adult ladybug is soft and pink. Its shell is not hard yet.

15

A convergent ladybug comes out of its case after about a week.

16 Once the shell hardens, a ladybug can fly. Its shell turns a bright color, such as red. Some ladybugs are orange or yellow. Others are dark colors such as brown or black instead.

Most adult ladybugs have spots on their shells. The two sides of the shell cover the ladybug's wings. Each part of the shell has the same number of spots.

17

About 500 species of ladybug live in the United States and Canada.

18

Spiders, tree frogs, and birds such as swallows and crows like to eat ladybugs.

Some ladybugs are **poisonous**. If a **predator** such as a bird picks up one of these ladybugs, it will get a really bad taste in its mouth. That is because the ladybug's legs release a bad-tasting gel. The gel can make a predator sick.

The color and spotted **pattern** of the shell let predators know that the ladybug may taste bad. Sometimes ladybugs also play dead if a predator is close by. They tuck their legs underneath their shell and stay very still.

A ladybug uses its feet as well as its antennae to pick up smells.

20   Ladybugs can live for a few months or up to three years. They eat mostly aphids and mites. They also eat white flies and **mealybugs**. A ladybug can eat up to 5,000 aphids in its short life!

To find bugs to eat, a ladybug uses its **antennae**. Two antennae stick out from the ladybug's head. They pick up scents, or smells, in the air. They also help a ladybug taste and feel its way around.

Most aphids do not have a way of keeping themselves safe from ladybugs.

Ladybugs can eat nectar from plants such as dandelions.

Some ladybugs feed on **nectar** from flowers. Others feed on **pollen**. Still other ladybug species eat plants or even mushrooms.

Ladybugs spend most of their time eating. They keep pests off plants. Most of the bugs ladybugs eat are harmful to plants. People who grow flowers or crops like having ladybugs around.

23

A ladybug's spots fade, or become lighter, as the ladybug gets older.

An adult ladybug looks for a mate. Male and female ladybugs give off scents that attract each other. These smells let other ladybugs know they are ready to mate.

Ladybugs often mate in the spring. Then the females lay their eggs right away. Sometimes ladybugs hold on to their eggs for two to three months.

25

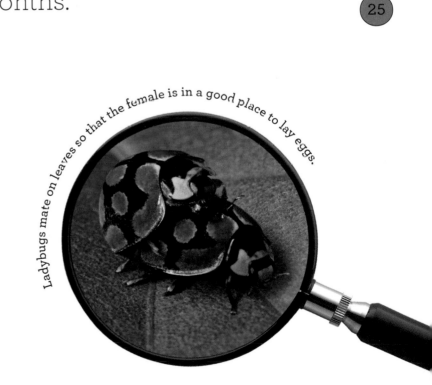

Ladybugs mate on leaves so that the female is in a good place to lay eggs.

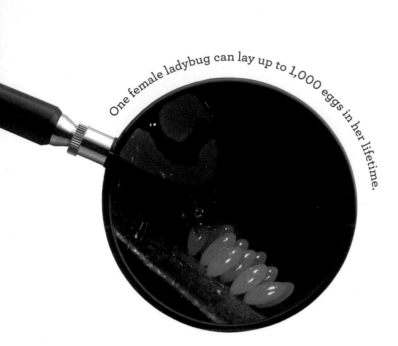

One female ladybug can lay up to 1,000 eggs in her lifetime.

26

Ladybugs that have long lives lay many egg clusters a year. Ladybugs like to spend the winter in warmer places, such as inside people's houses. Some ladybugs hide under leaves or rocks outside.

In the spring, when it is warmer, ladybugs come out again. They eat bugs and find mates. Then the females lay their eggs under a plant or on a leaf. A female chooses an egg-laying spot that is close to where the larvae will be able to find food.

Sometimes ladybugs will crowd together to find a new place to live.

27

As long as ladybugs are around, aphids cannot take over plants.

After one to three years, ladybugs get old and tired. When the males stop mating and the females stop laying eggs, they die. The larvae keep growing inside the eggs. These larvae will become pupae, and then they will turn into spotted ladybugs.

29

The ladybug lays her eggs on or under a leaf.

A larva begins growing in the egg.

The larva hatches from the egg in 3 to 7 days.

The larva sheds its skin 3 or 4 times.

At 2 to 4 weeks old, the larva is fully grown.

The larva changes into a  pupa at about 1 month old.

A pupa grows for 5 to 7 days to become an adult.

 The adult mates, and females lay eggs.

After 1 to 3 years, the ladybug dies.

30

antennae: *the pair of long, thin sense organs attached to a ladybug's head; "antenna" is the word for a single one*

aphids: *tiny insects with soft bodies that eat the sap (sugary water) made by plants*

larva: *the form a ladybug takes after it hatches but before it has skin and wings; "larvae" is the word for more than one larva*

mealybugs: *small insects coated with a powdery-white wax that feed on plant sap*

mites: *small arachnids (animals with eight legs that do not have a backbone) that live on plants and in the soil*

nectar: *a sweet, sugary liquid that flowers make*

pattern: *lines or shapes that are repeated*

permanent: *lasting for a long time*

poisonous: *causing death or illness*

pollen: *a yellow powder made by flowers that is used to fertilize other flowers*

predator: *an animal that kills and eats other animals*

pupa: *the form a ladybug takes as it changes from larva to adult; "pupae" is the word for more than one pupa*

species: *groups of living things that are closely related*

thorax: *the middle part of an insect's body, between the head and the abdomen*

31

WEB SITES

DLTK: Ladybugs Coloring Pages
http://www.coloring.ws/ladybugs1.htm
Download and print ladybug coloring pages.

Enchanted Learning: Ladybugs
http://www.enchantedlearning.com/subjects/insects/Ladybug.shtml
Print out pages to color and find instructions on how to make your own ladybug!

READ MORE

Allen, Judy. *Are You a Ladybug?*
New York: Kingfisher, 2000.

Marsico, Katie. *A Ladybug Larva Grows Up.*
New York: Children's Press, 2007.

32

INDEX